You Can Do a Puppet Show

Written and illustrated
by
Mike Harding

For my mom.

CONTENTS

Introduction

My name is Curtains. Let's learn how to do a puppet show.

The world needs more puppet shows. You can do them!

Think to yourself: What if I made
a puppet show?

What if, when you do a puppet show, you are like a wolf howling at the moon?

Let's spend some time together and learn how to make a puppet show.

Puppetry includes everything:

- Communicating
- Making things
- Writing
- Inventing
- Improvising
- Storytelling
- Painting
- Drawing
- Singing
- Comedy
- Engineering
- Playing
- Music
- Drama

  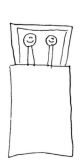

Step 1

Make Puppets!

Lots of things can be puppets.

- Socks
- Paper bags
- Your toys
- Things from around the house (add googly eye to almost anything!)
- Folded paper
- Sewn fabric

sock   fabric   paper   wrinkly lunch bag.

Make a hand puppet with two pieces of fabric, a marker, and glue. Trace your hand, cut out the shape and decorate!

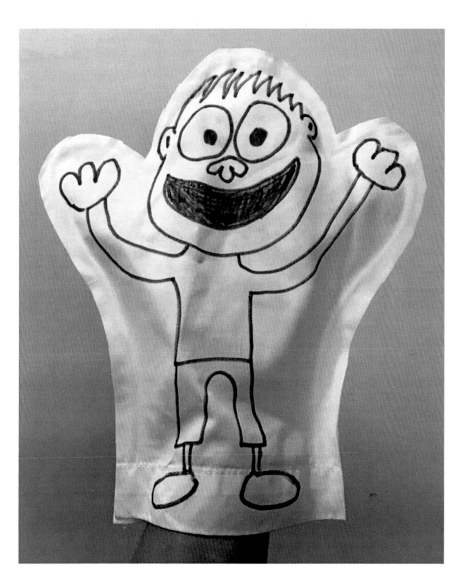

A fabric puppet that I made. You can use glue around the edge.

fold lengthwise into a long, skinny piece of paper.

fold in half into a "V"

fold the "V" into an "M"

put the puppet on your hand

decorate!

Make a puppet from a piece of paper.

Some paper puppets that I made.

This one has a body made
from rolled up paper.

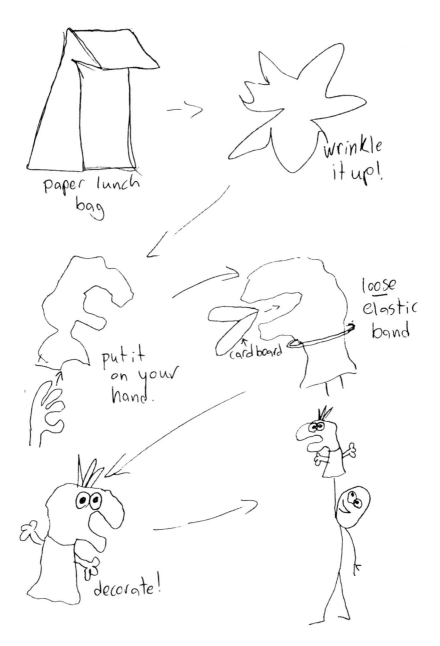

Make a puppet from a wrinkled lunch bag.

A wrinkled paper lunch bag
puppet that I made.

Make your puppet's eyes a little bit crossed.

Step 2

Make a Stage, Scenery, and Props!

For the Stage:

- Get a box
- Cut out an opening
- Make a curtain
- Decorate the box
- Hang your puppets inside

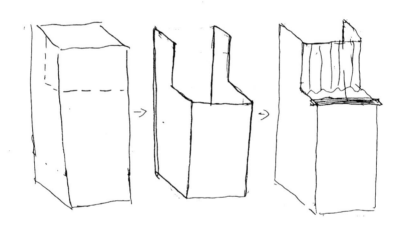

The puppet stage that I use.

Make Props and scenery out of cardboard.

popcycle stick

plastacine

string → ← hook
DANCE PARTY!

Step 3

Make a Story!

Start with these things:

① Character

② Thing

③ Mood

④ Place

⑤ Event

⑥ END? Ending (Optional)

Make your puppet show short. 3 to 5-minutes is enough. Make it simple but not boring.

Make the structure of your story look like a
roller coaster. Make good things and bad things
happen to the characters.

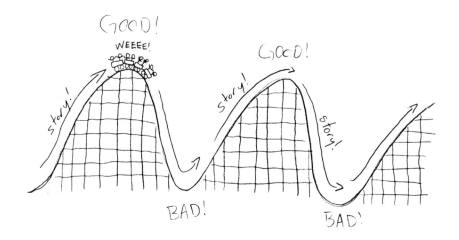

Have a beginning, middle, and end.

Where to find stories?

FAIRY TALES
(CHANGE THEM)
FROM BOOKS
+ TV SHOWS.

Ha Ha Ha!

TELL
JOKES!

SING
SONGS!

THESE ARE SHORT
STORIES!

MAKE UP YOUR
OWN STORY!

Step 4

Practice!

Pretend your puppet is walking on an imaginary floor. Always keep the puppet at the same height.

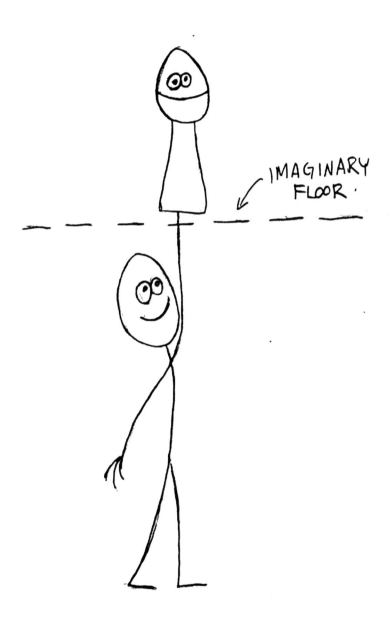

IMAGINARY FLOOR.

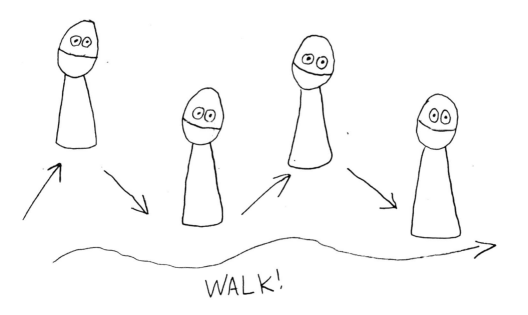

WALK!

Make your puppet walk or run along the
imaginary floor by bouncing the puppet
up and down.

Try not to rest your puppet on the puppet stage.
Hold it up.

Look at your puppet and learn where its eyes point. Try to make your puppet look at the audience.

Use your thumb more than your fingers when puppeteering. Make the puppet's jaw move more than its head.

Practice your puppet show in front of a mirror.

Record your puppet show on a phone and watch it later.

Step 5

Perform!

Sing a song or beat a drum to introduce your puppet show. Thank the audience for being there.

Make sure your audience knows where to sit.

Don't wait until your puppet
show is ready or perfect. Just
start. Mistakes are good and you
can learn from them.

"No one knows how the puppet show is
supposed to go except you."
~ Diane Harding (my Mom)

Maybe you can find a friend to do
puppet shows with you.

How much FUN the audience is having is more important than the puppet show.

Pay attention to the things that you LOVE
and get EXCITED about, add them to your
puppet shows.

Can you think of places where you can do your puppet show?

Make lots of mistakes and have fun. The world needs more puppet shows!

My name is Mike and I love doing puppet shows. I started making puppets when I was about 10 years old. In high school I made some really great puppets but I needed something to do with them so I started performing in bookstores. When people saw my puppet shows they would sometimes ask me to perform at birthday parties, libraries, and schools. Now doing puppet shows is my job!

Have fun!

Take a photo or video of your puppet show and tag @applefun-puppetry!

You can watch examples of my puppet shows and puppetry workshops on YouTube. Just scan here:

Thank you for reading this book. I hope that you loved it! Can you leave a review on Amazon? It would help a lot!

Manufactured by Amazon.ca
Acheson, AB

14614665R00033